THE SECOND WORLD WAR IN THE AIR IN PHOTOGRAPHS

1944

L. ARCHARD

First published 2015

Amberley Publishing
The Hill, Stroud
Gloucestershire, GL5 4EP

www.amberley-books.com

British Library Cataloguing in Publication Data.
A catalogue record for this book is available from the British Library.

ISBN 978 1 4456 2251 4 (print)
ISBN 978 1 4456 2274 3 (ebook)

Typesetting and Origination by Amberley Publishing.
Printed in Great Britain.

Contents

Acknowledgements

I would like to take this opportunity to thank John Christopher for making images of the Me 262 from his collection available to me for this book.

Introduction

The war in the air in 1944 began much as 1943 had ended as the RAF bombing campaign against Berlin that had begun in November 1943 continued. On 20 January, for example, Bomber Command dropped 2,300 tons of bombs on the German capital. On the Italian front, January saw the British Army's X Corps along the Garigliano River, at the western end of the Gustav Line, a German defensive position constructed across the width of the Italian peninsula. The town of Cassino, and the historic Benedictine monastery that overlooked it from the top of the mountain of Monte Cassino, was a key point in the Gustav Line. Allied officers were convinced that the Germans were using the abbey as an observation point to direct their artillery fire onto the attacking troops. On 15 February, 142 B-17 Flying Fortresses as well as Mitchell and Marauder bombers dropped more than 1,100 tons of high explosive and incendiary bombs onto the abbey. The rubble created by the bombing and the artillery fire that was also directed onto the abbey made it an ideal defensive position for the German fallschirmjäger, regardless of whether they had been occupying it previously. It would be May before the Battle of Monte Cassino was finally over.

The week of 20–25 February was Big Week for the USAAF, a series of bombing missions flown largely by the Eighth Air Force in Britain, but also by the Fifteenth Air Force from its bases in Italy. Throughout 1943, the Eighth Air Force had been flying missions over Germany, relying on the heavy defensive armament of the B-17s and B-24s to protect them from German fighters when they were out of the range of the escorting P-47s and P-38s. However, the losses, particularly in the raids against Schweinfurt and Regensburg, were unsustainable. What changed this situation was the arrival of large numbers of P-51 Mustangs, which had the range to escort the bombers to their targets and back. The losses on the Big Week raids, even when the bomber crews went back to targets such as Schweinfurt and Regensburg, were a far smaller percentage of the force than they had been before the arrival of the Mustangs.

As the fighting around Monte Cassino continued into March, the town of Cassino itself was also destroyed from the air by Allied heavy bombers. 750 tons of 1,000-lb bombs with delayed action fuses were dropped on the town in the hope that it would help New Zealand troops push the German paratroopers out.

April 1944 saw Japanese forces in China launch Operation Ichi-Go, which aimed, among other things, to capture airbases in south-western China that the USAAF had been using to stage raids by B-29 bombers against Japanese forces in China, Thailand and Burma. On 15 June, B-29s flying from airbases around Chengdu in Sichuan Province carried out the first air raid on the Japanese home islands since the Doolittle Raid of 1942 when they attacked a steel works on the southern island of Kyushu.

On 6 June, the Western Allies opened the long-awaited second front, landing at five invasion beaches along a 50-mile stretch of the Normandy coast. The invasion, codenamed Operation Overlord, was the largest amphibious operation in history, with over 150,000 men involved. Included in that total were 24,000 airborne troops, who landed behind the beaches shortly after midnight on 6 June. Over 13,000 men of the US 101st and 82nd airborne divisions landed by parachute and, later, glider behind Utah beach and around the River Douve. The paratroopers successfully destroyed bridges over the River Douve and captured the crossroads at Sainte-Mère-Église, the first town to be liberated in the invasion. This was despite problems with the marking of the drop zones and with the navigation of the transport aircraft that dropped the paratroopers, caused by heavy cloud over Normandy. On the British side, a glider assault by 5th Parachute Brigade and 7th (Light Infantry) Parachute Battalion captured Pegasus Bridge over the Caen Canal and Horsa Bridge over the Orne River. However, the British paratroopers suffered from the weather as the Americans had, being blown off course and landing too far east.

As well as the landing of airborne troops, the Allied air forces played a key role before, during and immediately after D-Day. Over 2,000 RAF and USAAF bombers attacked targets along the Normandy coast and inland from the invasion beaches at about midnight. On Utah beach, the USAAF bombers had come in at a lower altitude than they had been briefed to fly at and were able to cause heavy damage to the defences. On Omaha, by contrast, the bombers had had to delay dropping their bombs to avoid hitting the landing craft, leaving many of the defences and obstacles undamaged. Over the coming days, Allied fighter bombers and light bombers, flying from bases on the south coast of England and marked with distinctive black and white stripes on their wings and tails to prevent friendly fire from troops on the ground, flew countless missions in support of the troops on the ground and destroyed the bridges and crossroads needed by the Germans to transport reinforcements to Normandy, especially the Panzer divisions.

On 13 June, a week after the D-Day landings, and in direct response to them, Hitler ordered the launch of the first V-1 Flying Bomb against Britain; that first V-1 landed next to a railway bridge on Grove Road, in the Mile End district of London. The V-1 had been in development since the start of the war, the first test flights at the research station at Peenemünde on the Baltic coast coming in late 1942. Powered by a simple pulse jet engine, the buzzing noise of which gave rise to the nickname Buzz Bomb, the V-1 also used a simple autopilot system to control its speed and altitude. An anemometer in the nose counted down a certain number of turns (based on the prevailing wind speed) and when it reached zero a mechanism was set off that set the V-1's rudder in neutral and caused it to make a steep dive onto the target. This process cut off the power to the engine, so civilians on the ground quickly learned to listen for the buzzing sound and take cover when it stopped. V-1 attacks, against both London and targets in liberated Europe such as the Belgian port of Antwerp, would continue through the rest of 1944 and into 1945. At the peak of the V-1 offensive, almost 100 were being launched per day against the south-east of England, almost 10,000 in total. Almost 2,500 reached London, killing more than 6,000 people and injuring almost another 18,000. Antwerp was hit by almost 2,500 more V-1s. To this casualty list have to be added concentration camp inmates worked to death in the Mittelwerk underground factory at Nordhausen, where both V-1 Flying Bombs and V-2 rockets were produced between 1943 and 1945. Barrage balloons, anti-aircraft fire and manned fighters – particularly the Hawker Tempest, but also P-51 Mustangs, Spitfire Mk XIVs and de Havilland Mosquitoes – were all effective defences against the V-1.

Later in June, the US and Japanese navies fought the last of the major carrier battles in the Pacific, the Battle of the Philippine Sea, in the waters off the Mariana Islands. The Marianas were important to the Japanese for protecting the islands of Japan itself as well as the sea lanes leading to them. Between 19 and 20 June, the Japanese lost three of their fleet carriers to American submarines and naval aircraft, the *Taihō*, *Shōkaku* and *Hiyo*, as well as hundreds of aircraft and aircrew, a result so one-sided that the battle became known to the Americans as the 'Great Marianas Turkey Shoot'. The Japanese had lost 90 per cent of the carrier air groups that they had spent the best part of a year building up, and the losses were irreplaceable; in the Battle of Leyte Gulf in October, the Japanese had so few pilots that the carriers could only be used as decoys. The Battle of Leyte Gulf, the largest naval battle of the Second World War (and possibly the largest in history), came as the Japanese attempted to stop the American invasion of Leyte, the largest of the Philippine islands. It was also the first battle in which the Japanese carried out organised Kamikaze attacks against the American fleet, sinking one of the escort carriers, USS *St Lo*, and damaging several others. These were the first attacks by pilots of the Special Attack Group; other Japanese pilots also carried out Kamikaze attacks during the invasion of Leyte, causing damage to the heavy cruiser HMAS *Australia* among others.

At the end of July, a Luftwaffe pilot flying a Messerschmitt Me 262 scored the first aerial victory by a jet fighter, attacking and damaging an RAF Mosquito reconnaissance aircraft. The Me 262 had been under development since 1939, when the first plans were drawn up for the aircraft, and the first operational unit flying the Me 262 came into service in April 1944. Me 262s, particularly those armed with rockets, were lethally effective against Allied bombers, as they were too fast and could climb too quickly for the escorting propeller-driven fighters to intercept them. As the German pilots worked out the best tactics to use with the Me 262, it also became very effective in shooting down the Allied fighters. One tactic that was used successfully against the Me 262s was for RAF Hawker Tempests to attack them at low level as they came into land at their base, but the Germans set up flak defences that quickly caused such high losses among the Tempest pilots that this was stopped.

The V-2, the world's first long-range ballistic missile, was developed by Dr Werner von Braun and his research team from the 1930s onwards, and its manufacture and deployment were ordered by Hitler to help maintain German civilian morale in the face of the Allied bombing of German cities. From September 1944, more than 3,000 V-2s were launched at London, Antwerp and Liège, causing some 9,000 deaths in addition to all those who had died at the Mittelwerk factory. Unlike the V-1, the V-2 was very difficult to intercept in flight and so the main countermeasure that could be taken was the destruction of the infrastructure used to launch the rockets. The rocket itself was fuelled by a mixture of ethanol and water with a liquid oxygen oxidiser; the first models used a simple analogue computer to calculate the angle of flight needed to hit the target but some later ones were guided by radio signals from the ground. Radio control was also used to determine when to cut off power to the engines.

On 17 September, Operation Market Garden began, Field Marshal Montgomery's daring plan to outflank the defensive positions along the German border by outflanking the Siegfried Line, crossing the Rhine north of where the Line finished. In what was the largest airborne operation ever up until that point, over 40,000 British and American airborne troops were dropped into the Netherlands to capture the bridges over the Rhine, the Maas and several tributaries and canals. Although several of the bridges between Eindhoven and Nijmegen were captured, the ground troops from the British XXX Corps made slower progress than expected and the paratroopers from the British 1st Airborne Division who had landed around the bridge at Arnhem faced stronger resistance than had been anticipated. Although the paratroopers managed to reach the bridge, they were pushed back to the west bank of the Rhine by German forces including men from the 9th and 10th SS panzer divisions, and on 25 September the surviving British paratroopers were pulled back behind the Allied lines.

By November, V-2 rockets were hitting Britain at the rate of around eight every day. On 12 November, the RAF finally succeeded in putting an end to one of Churchill's bugbears and sank the battleship *Tirpitz*. Modified Lancasters of 617 Squadron and 9 Squadron carrying 12,000-lb Tallboy earthquake bombs attacked *Tirpitz*, achieving two direct hits and a near miss. A hit amidships led to flooding that caused a list on *Tirpitz* that increased to as much as 40 degrees and the order was given to abandon ship. Not long after, an explosion rocked the ship and caused her to capsize. The Lancasters of 617 Squadron and 9 Squadron had made two attempts, in mid-September and at the end of October, to sink *Tirpitz* with Tallboy bombs after the failure of the Royal Navy to sink her, including attacks by aircraft of the Fleet Air Arm and by midget submarines.

In mid-December, the Germans launched a surprise attack against American forces in the Ardennes Forest in Belgium, aiming to reach the port of Antwerp, stopping its use as a supply base and splitting the Allied forces in the West in two. Hitler believed that the Germans could then encircle and destroy the Allied forces separately, forcing the Western Allies to negotiate a separate peace, allowing him to concentrate on the fight against the USSR. The German attack was launched in heavily overcast weather conditions, which meant that the Allies could not bring their air power to bear. By 21 December, the Germans had surrounded Bastogne, which was defended by paratroopers from the American 101st Airborne Division. Improved weather conditions over the next few days allowed the Allied air forces to drop supplies to the besieged American paratroopers in Bastogne and to attack the German troops and their supply lines, bringing the offensive to a halt. In the Far East, the continuing Japanese Ichi-Go offensive led to a request for the bombing of the Chinese city of Hankow, a supply centre for the Japanese troops. On 18 December, eighty-four B-29s attacked the city with 500 tons of incendiary bombs; Hankow, a largely wooden city, burned for three days after the raid. This was one of the last B-29 raids launched from the bases in China, which were extremely difficult to supply as fuel, spare parts and everything else required to fly missions needed to be flown in over the Himalayas from India. From the start of 1945, the B-29s would instead fly from bases on the Mariana Islands and after the effectiveness of the raid on Hankow, fire-bombing would soon be used against the cities of Japan, which were also largely wooden.

Although the war in the air in 1944 demonstrated that the Axis powers were still capable of surprising the Allies, the Kamikaze attacks and the German jet and rocket technology in particular, the overwhelming Allied superiority in numbers and in industrial production of aircraft, ships and other weapons, munitions, and so on meant that an Allied victory was now only a matter of time. The failure of Operation Market Garden, however, meant that relatively easy options were not necessarily likely to reduce the amount of time that it would take to achieve victory.

January

Bombs exploding in the town of Orsogna, near the Adriatic coast of the Abruzzo in central Italy.

An artist's impression of massed B-17 Flying Fortresses under attack from German fighters during a large-scale raid over Germany by the Eighth Air Force on 11 January.

A more realistic image: a photograph showing sixty-eight B-24s and B-17s, vapour trails streaming in their wake, on their way to their targets in Germany.

A B-17, flames pouring from its port side, loses height after coming under attack from a Fw 190 on 11 January.

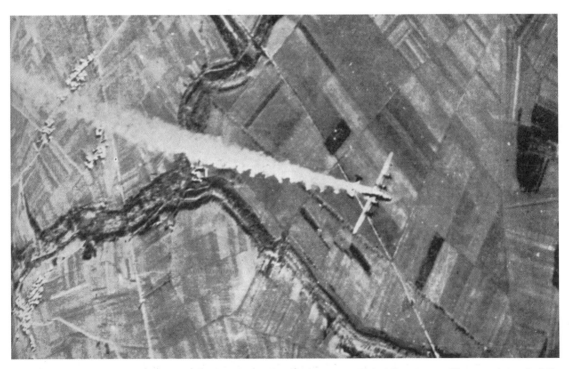

B-24 Liberators were also involved in the raids of 11 January. This Liberator, trailing smoke as it falls to the ground, was hit by anti-aircraft fire over Germany.

An Avro Lancaster Mk I of Bomber Command sits with its engines running, ready to take off for a raid over Germany.

A WAAF radio operator sits in the flying control room of one of the Bomber Command airfields, ready to guide the aircraft back in on their return.

By contrast, this photograph shows the flying control tower on a jungle airfield in the north of Australia, where the control officer is using a lamp to flash a signal to a fighter pilot that he is clear to land.

A US Marine, wounded in a landing in the Gilbert Islands, is taken out by boat to a flying boat that will transport him and other wounded men to a hospital base. Over the vast distances of the Pacific, air ambulances could be vitally important.

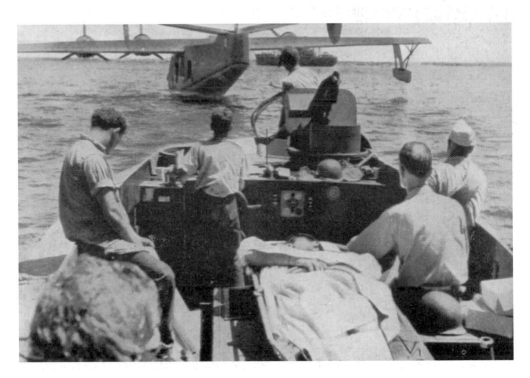

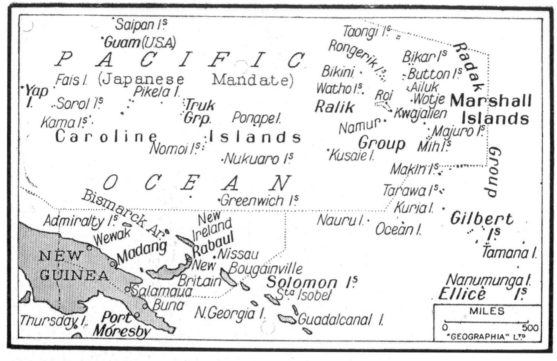

The south-west Pacific, showing New Guinea, the Solomon Islands, the Gilbert Islands and Guam and Saipan, among other island groups.

A look-out on a US Navy warship in the Pacific watches an Essex-class aircraft carrier. The Essex class was the backbone of the US carrier force during the Second World War and for some years after, twenty-four being built.

A flak tower off the east coast of England, garrisoned by Royal Marines and RNVR officers and equipped with anti-aircraft guns to defend shipping from air attack.

There were also flak towers on land. This example was part of the defences of Dover against Luftwaffe raiders flying from bases in northern France.

Loading an Avro Lancaster Mk 2 for a raid against a German city. The ground crew are loading 500-lb high explosive bombs; a 4,000-lb bomb and several bundles of incendiaries can also be seen in the bomb bay. Standard loads of high explosive and incendiary bombs were developed to make raids as destructive and effective as possible.

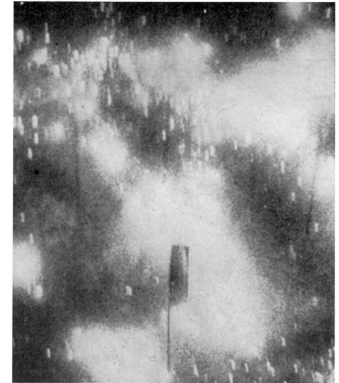

A 4,000-lb bomb drops from the bomb bay of an RAF bomber over Magdeburg in eastern Germany during a raid on 21 January.

A bombing raid by B-25 Mitchell bombers of the USAAF on Civitavecchia harbour. Allied aircraft were particularly active in Italy to support the Anzio landings, just south of Rome, on 22 January.

Another photograph of the air war over Italy; this raid, also carried out by American Mitchell bombers, hit marshalling yards just north of Rome to make the movement of troops towards the front line more difficult.

Members of the VAD (Voluntary Aid Detachment, a volunteer nursing organisation) and others are seen here watching a demonstration of how to unbuckle the parachute of a crashed airman.

February

A U-boat sunk in early 1944 by a Short Sunderland flying boat sinks by the stern as the crew scramble to escape out of the conning tower.

A B-17 Flying Fortress of RAF Coastal Command about to take off from the Azores on patrol.
RAF Flying Fortresses would claim eleven U-boats destroyed during the war.

A store of petrol for the aircraft flying out of the Azores on anti-submarine patrols.

A US Navy aircraft carrier, with one of its destroyer escorts visible behind it, moves on as a Japanese torpedo bomber crashes into the sea to the right of this photograph. The aircraft launched an attack on the carrier as it returned from the US invasion of the Marshall Islands.

The hill-top medieval Benedictine abbey of Monte Cassino is seen in the top left of this photograph. Fearing that it had been turned into a strongpoint by the occupying Germans, the Allies asked the permission of the Pope before bombing the abbey.

The ruins of the abbey of Monte Cassino following the Allied bombing attack.

A Junkers Ju 52 dropping food and other supplies to German troops trapped in a pocket on the Eastern Front.

Trucks on fire in the Anzio beachhead in Italy following an attack by the Luftwaffe.

On 18 February 1944, the RAF launched Operation Jericho. Eighteen Mosquitoes from 464 Squadron RAAF, 487 Squadron RNZAF and 21 Squadron RAF flew a low-level raid against Amiens Prison to release political prisoners and members of the French Resistance being held there. The Mosquito pilots bombed the guardhouse and blew breaches in the walls of the prison, allowing over 250 prisoners to escape. One of the breaches in the wall can be seen to the right of this photograph.

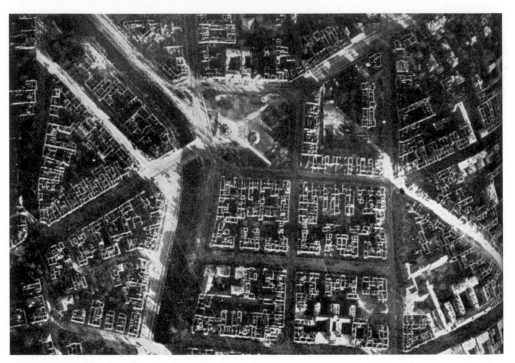

An area of central Berlin south of the Tiergarten and east of the Zoological Gardens badly damaged by Allied air attacks on the city; the vast majority of the buildings are roofless. Between November 1943 and February 1944, there was a concerted offensive against Berlin by Bomber Command and the US Eighth Air Force that destroyed large parts of the city. In the map below, heavy damage or complete destruction are indicated by a blacked-out area, including in the area shown in the photograph.

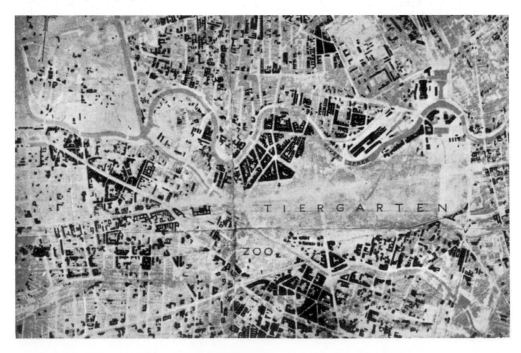

On 20 February, B-17 Flying Fortresses of the Eighth Air Force attacked a plant in Leipzig making components for the Messerschmitt Bf 109 fighter. These two photographs show the attack on Leipzig, but on that day the Eighth Air Force also attacked aircraft industry targets in Gotha, Bernberg and Brunswick among others.

Ground crew loading boxes with belts of ammunition for the machine guns on board a B-24 Liberator. Some of the different kinds of bombs carried by the Liberator can be seen in the foreground of the photograph.

Mechanics working on a Coastal Command Liberator that has not long returned from a long-range patrol. In order to maintain air cover over the North Atlantic, constant maintenance of aircraft was required.

Commanders of the Allied air forces planning the air offensive against occupied Europe. How to support the forthcoming D-Day landings and the deception operation to convince the Germans the landing would be in the Pas de Calais would have been key considerations.

A reconnaissance photograph showing Stuttgart very soon after a raid on the city by RAF Bomber Command. To the top right, smoke is rising from the Robert Bosch works, where magnetos and ignition equipment, vital for both military aircraft and ground vehicles, was manufactured.

The wrecked airfield on the atoll of Roi in the Marshall Islands.

March

B-17s of the Eighth Air Force flying through bursts of black smoke from anti-aircraft fire over Berlin on 6 March 1944.

Bombs dropped by the Eighth Air Force bombers exploding on their targets during the raids on 6 March.

A B-17 flying over the ball bearing plant in the Berlin suburb of Erkner, which was attacked by the Eighth Air Force on 8 March.

On 15 March, Allied bombers launched a mass attack against the town of Cassino, at the foot of the mountain of Monte Cassino. These two photographs show the rubble of the town after the attack.

Clearing the snow off the runways and taxiways of a Bomber Command airfield using a device that seems to be the forerunner of the equipment used to clear runways on airports now.

However, the bad weather conditions did not necessarily mean that operations would be suspended. A line of Lancaster bombers on a snowy airfield are being prepared for a raid, with a 4,000-lb bomb in front of the second aircraft in the line.

An artist's impression of troops of the 14th Army being supplied by an airdrop as they advance through the jungle towards the Chindwin River. The 'L' shape made using flares to mark the drop point for the aircraft can be seen to the left.

The area around the border of India and Burma (now Myanmar), showing the Chindwin River and the city of Mandalay.

An RAF Bomber Command aircrew walk away from their aircraft after returning from a raid on Frankfurt on 19 March.

The 12,000-lb Tallboy bomb, designed by Barnes Wallis, started to come into service with RAF Bomber Command in 1944. The bomb was designed to burrow into the earth and then explode, creating an earthquake effect that would destroy the foundations of the target.

Two photographs showing Marauder B26 bombers in Europe. The first image shows 1,000-lb bombs falling from Marauders of the US Twelfth Air Force onto Piombino, 105 miles north-west of Rome. The second photograph shows Marauders attacking a Luftwaffe airfield in the Netherlands.

A big group of bombs falling on the Dornier Werke assembly and repair plant at Oberpfaffenhofen in southern Germany during a raid by the US Eighth Air Force on 18 March.

Boats on the Irrawaddy River being used by the Japanese, probably to transport petrol or fuel, on fire after having been attacked by RAF aircraft.

A series of three photographs showing a Messerschmitt Bf 109G being shot down as it takes off from an airfield in northern France by an RAF Hawker Typhoon fighter. The first photograph shows the Bf 109G taking off while the second and third show impacts on the fuselage and port wing from the Typhoon's cannon fire.

A convoy off the Friesian Islands, along the Dutch and German coasts, under attack by Bristol Beaufighters carrying torpedoes.

April

At dawn on 3 April, a force of forty-two Fleet Air Arm Barracuda torpedo bombers launched an attack on the battleship *Tirpitz* at her anchorage in Altenfjord on the Norwegian coast. This photograph shows some of the crews being briefed before taking off.

Part of the force of Barracudas flying over the Norwegian fjords en route to Altenfjord and the *Tirpitz*.

A cloud of smoke rises from the *Tirpitz* after the first wave of Barracudas has made its attack.

The escort carrier HMS *Pursuer* provided fighter cover for the attack with her Grumman Wildcat fighters. Later in the month, Wildcat fighters from the *Pursuer* attacked a German supply convoy off Bodo on the Norwegian coast. These two photographs show a fighter taking off and a more general view of the flight deck.

On 8 April, Vickers Wellington bombers escorted by Spitfire fighters attacked Niksic in what was then Yugoslavia at the request of the Yugoslav partisan leader, Tito.

B-24 Liberators of the Fifteenth Air Force flying towards Wiener Neustadt in Austria to attack the Messerschmitt factory there on 12 April.

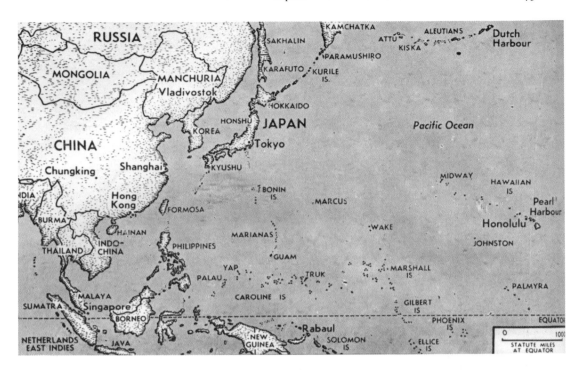

The Pacific theatre of the war from Hawaii and the Aleutian Islands to India and Burma and the islands of what is now Indonesia.

A white phosphorus bomb exploding on the Japanese airfield at Lakunai, Rabaul, on the island of New Britain.

A US Navy Avenger torpedo bomber making an attack on a Japanese destroyer at the naval base in Truk.

Smoke rises up from explosions from bombs dropped by US Navy carrier aircraft during an air raid on a Japanese base on the island of Saipan in the Marianas.

An attack by aircraft of the US Fifth Air Force on a Japanese airfield at Hollandia in the north-east of New Guinea.

A B-24 Liberator during an attack on railway yards and repair shops at Vinh in what was then French Indo-China but which is now the north of Vietnam.

Ground crew examine damage sustained by a Lancaster bomber from a Luftwaffe night fighter's cannon fire over Düsseldorf on 22 April.

A factory outside Oslo in occupied Norway, which was being used to repair Fw 190s, Me 109s and Ju 52s was attacked by Bomber Command on 28 April.

A B-17 Flying Fortress photographed from below while over the target, its bomb bay doors open prior to dropping its load of bombs, which are clearly visible.

On 29 April, the Eighth Air Force mounted a raid of some 1,500 bombers against Berlin, 'Big B' as the American airmen knew the city. In this photograph, a B-17 can be seen over Tempelhof airfield.

German soldiers unloading a transport aircraft that had carried supplies into a pocket of German troops trapped by a Soviet offensive in the western Ukraine.

May

On 5 May, the Pescara Dam was attacked by P-51 Mustang fighters and P-40 Kittyhawk dive bombers. A breach was made in the dam, flooding many of the nearby valleys.

On 10 May, B-17 Flying Fortresses of the US Fifteenth Air Force flying from bases in Italy attacked the Messerschmitt factory at Wiener Neustadt, just outside Vienna, a major centre for the production of Bf 109 fighters.

Above left: Female workers in Australia producing ammunition on turret lathes.

Above right: Bombs are unloaded from a cargo ship in an un-named port in the eastern Mediterranean. Munitions, an obviously dangerous cargo, had to be moved in vast quantities across the world to keep the fighting forces supplied.

Right: Two British soldiers pose with the casing of a Butterfly bomb, an early cluster bomb used by the Germans from 1940 onwards, in the Blitz, on the Eastern Front and in the Mediterranean.

Three photographs taken in Berlin by a
Swiss photographer and showing from
the ground the devastation that had been
inflicted on the Nazi capital between
November 1943 and March 1944.

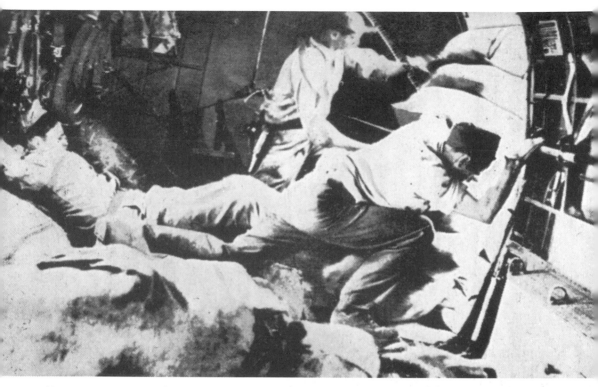

Air transport was used to keep the armies advancing through northern Burma supplied without slowing the ground troops down. These two photographs show supplies being dropped by parachute and a reluctant mule being loaded into a transport aircraft. In the jungles of Burma, mules were often more effective transport than lorries.

Two views of the Martin factory at Offut, Nebraska, one of four plants where the B-29 Superfortress bomber was assembled. The top picture shows the production line and the second shows one of the giant bombers in the open air outside the plant. (LoC)

Two photographs showing a U-boat in the Atlantic under attack from a Sunderland flying boat of the Royal Canadian Air Force. The top image shows depth charges exploding around the submarine while the bottom image shows the crew scrambling to escape from the conning tower.

Bombs explode on a Japanese base in the Marshall Islands as a US B-25 Mitchell bomber of the Seventh Air Force turns back into formation during an air raid.

This photograph was taken in Terracina, on the coast south of Rome and at the southern end of the ancient Appian Way, after its occupation by Allied forces on 24 May. It shows shipping wrecked by Allied air attacks in the Terracina Canal.

A German supply convoy in the Soviet Union attacked by the Soviet Air Force during an offensive.

A formation of Petlyakov Pe-2 dive bombers of the Soviet Air Force. The Pe-2 was very widely used by the Soviet Air Force and carried a crew of three or four and a bomb load of around 1,300 lb.

General Montgomery visiting an aircraft carrier of the Royal Navy's Home Fleet and examining the Mae West life jacket of one of the pilots. The Mae West, commonly issued to both US and British aircrew, was an inflatable life preserver invented in 1928 and got its name because when inflated, the wearer apparently resembled the well-endowed American actress Mae West.

June

On 6 June 1944, Operation Overlord saw the invasion of Normandy by over 150,000 Allied troops. A key part of the invasion was the landing behind the invasion beaches of 24,000 British, Canadian and American airborne troops. In this photograph, a small part of the glider-borne forces can be seen flying over the Royal Navy battleships *Warspite* and *Ramillies* and an escorting destroyer.

General Eisenhower, the Supreme Commander of Allied Forces Europe, talks to paratroopers with blacked faces before they board their transport aircraft for the trip to Normandy.

British Hamilcar gliders coming into land in Normandy. The Hamilcar was a large glider designed by the British to carry heavy equipment like 17-pounder anti-tank guns and light reconnaissance tanks for the airborne forces.

Waco gliders used by the American airborne divisions in Normandy. Two American divisions were dropped into Normandy, the 101st and the 82nd, alongside the British 6th Airborne.

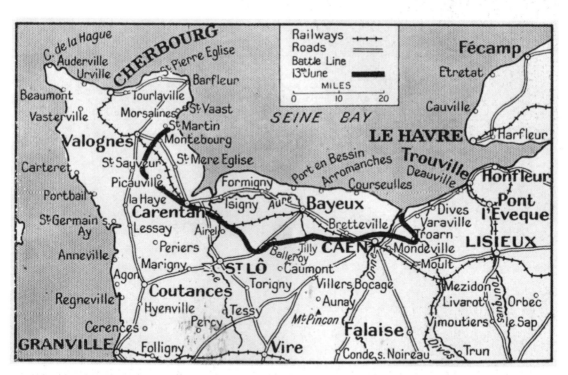

A map of Normandy showing the strip of coastline where the invasion took place, and the front line on 13 June, a week after the invasion.

Bombs dropped by aircraft of the US Eighth Air Force explode around a bridge on the River Loire east of Tours in order to prevent German forces from elsewhere in France being moved to Normandy to fight the invasion forces.

Two posters encouraging American women to take up jobs in the factories that were producing aircraft and other weapons of war for the armed forces. (LoC)

Mrs Angeline Kwint, whose husband and son were in the US Army, making fuel trailer tanks for the USAAF at the Heil Company in Milwaukee, Wisconsin. (LoC)

Metal tubing at the Consolidated Aircraft plant in Fort Worth, Texas. (LoC)

Fuelling an SNC advanced training plane at Corpus Christi Naval Air Base, Texas. (LoC)

A worker inside the nose of a PBY Catalina flying boat. (LoC)

A US Navy Aviation Ordnanceman tests a machine gun that he has just fitted to an aircraft at Corpus Christi Naval Air Base, Texas. (LoC)

Student pilots examining a map beside one of the training aircraft at Meacham Field outside Fort Worth, Texas. (LoC)

An instructor explains how a parachute works to a group of student pilots at Meacham Field, Fort Worth. (LoC)

B-17 *I'll Get By* of the 95th Bomb Group, 412th Bomb Squadron, which was shot down on 8 February 1944. (USAF)

A line-up of P-51 Mustang fighters on an airfield. It was the arrival of the P-51 in large numbers in the European Theatre of Operations that allowed the US Eighth Air Force to mount missions like Big Week in late February without the casualties that had resulted from earlier operations. (USAF)

P-51s of the 361st Fighter Group over France, 20 July 1944. (USAF)

Two officers from the 381st Bomb Group sit in the mess at their base at Ridgewell, Essex, in January 1944. (USAF)

Two armourers loading machine-gun ammunition into the wings of a P-51 Mustang. (USAF)

A pile of equipment needed for a P-51 mission over Europe – extra fuel tanks, bombs and machine-gun ammunition. (USAF)

Nine crewmen pose in front of their B-24 Liberator bomber. (USAF)

A crewman places fuses into the noses of bombs in the bomb bay of an Eighth Air Force bomber. (USAF)

Crewmen check the bombs on a trolley parked next to a B-17 Flying Fortress on a base somewhere in East Anglia while other crewmen check the engine and nose of the aircraft itself. (USAF)

Cheerful-looking Eighth Air Force aircrew pose for the camera before flying a mission in support of the D-Day invasion forces in June 1944. (USAF)

A female farm worker pauses with a sheaf of hay in her arms in a field next to an Eighth Air Force base, the wings of the B-17 aircraft jutting over the low, ivy-covered wall. (USAF)

Students and instructors at Meacham Field, Fort Worth. (LoC)

Bridges over the Seine at Rouen, bombed by the RAF following the D-Day landings.

The silhouette of a V-1 Flying Bomb in flight. The first V-1 attack on London was launched on 13 June, in response to the D-Day landings a week previously.

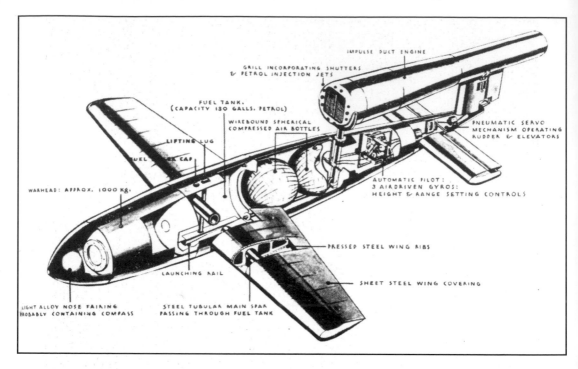

IMPULSE DUCT ENGINE

GRILL INCORPORATING SHUTTERS
& PETROL INJECTION JETS

FUEL TANK.
(CAPACITY 130 GALLS. PETROL)

WIREBOUND SPHERICAL
COMPRESSED AIR BOTTLES

PNEUMATIC SERVO
MECHANISM OPERATING
RUDDER & ELEVATORS

LIFTING LUG

FUEL TANK CAP

AUTOMATIC PILOT:
3 AIRDRIVEN GYROS:
HEIGHT & RANGE SETTING CONTROLS

WARHEAD: APPROX. 1000 Kg.

PRESSED STEEL WING RIBS

LAUNCHING RAIL

SHEET STEEL WING COVERING

LIGHT ALLOY NOSE FAIRING
PROBABLY CONTAINING COMPASS

STEEL TUBULAR MAIN SPAR
PASSING THROUGH FUEL TANK

A cutaway diagram showing the inside of the V-1. The sound of the Argus pulse jet engine led to the nick-name 'Buzz bomb'. The V-1 was guided to its target by a simple autopilot, labelled towards the rear in this diagram. At first, when the V-1 dived onto its target the fuel supply to the engine was cut off, so those on the ground learned to listen for the sound.

Two views of a V-1 launch site; both these photographs show sites in northern France but V-1s were launched from the coast of the Netherlands as well. In the lower image, the camouflaged launch ramp for the V-1 can be clearly seen.

Left: One solution to the problem of the Flying Bombs: smoke rises from bombs dropped by aircraft of the Eighth Air Force on a V-1 launch site. These missions were code-named No Ball by the Americans.

Below: Anti-aircraft gunfire could also be an effective defence against the Flying Bombs. This photograph shows a V-1 exploding over the Channel in a barrage of anti-aircraft fire.

Fighters could also intercept and destroy the V-1s. This artist's impression shows Spitfires in action against Flying Bombs over the Channel coast, but Hawker Tempests and Typhoons were also used, as were P-51 Mustangs.

Despite the defences, V-1s of course got through and hit London and the South East, the greatest density falling in Croydon, to the south-east of London. In response, children were evacuated from the South East, out of range of the Flying Bombs.

An artist's impression of rocket-firing RAF Hawker Typhoon fighter bombers attacking German tanks drawn up in a Normandy orchard. Seventeen of the twenty-five tanks were claimed as destroyed by the pilots in this attack.

Arming a Typhoon with rockets. The Typhoon, made by Hawker and designed by Sydney Camm as a successor to his very successful Hurricane, carried a 2,200 hp Napier Sabre engine and four 20-mm cannon in addition to the eight 60-lb rockets or two bombs.

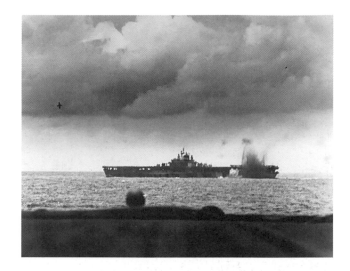

Three images from the Battle of the Philippine Sea, which was fought between 19 and 20 June. The top image shows a near miss by a Japanese bomb aimed at the aircraft carrier USS *Bunker Hill* on 19 June. The middle image shows US Navy fighter pilot Alex Vraciu signalling that he had shot down six Japanese dive bombers during what became known as the 'Great Marianas Turkey Shoot'. The bottom image shows the Japanese aircraft carrier *Zuikaku* and two escorting destroyers manoeuvring as they are attacked by US Navy carrier aircraft. (US Navy)

July

A Handley Page Halifax bomber over its target, described as a 'large concrete structure', in the Pas de Calais in northern France on 6 July.

Another air raid over the Pas de Calais on 6 July, this time showing a V-1 launch site under attack by aircraft of the Eighth Air Force.

A Spitfire Mk XI used for photo-reconnaissance missions shows off the black and white stripes used to help distinguish Allied aircraft following the Normandy invasion.

A train being used to carry supplies for the Japanese forces in Burma is concealed by plumes of dust and smoke from exploding cannon shells as it is strafed by an RAF Bristol Beaufighter.

A Lancaster bomber flies over the smoke cloud covering the historic Norman city of Caen. Heavy bombing raids on the night of 7/8 July and the morning of 8 July were intended to keep the German forces in the city from retreating, stop reinforcements arriving and clear the path of the Allied troops advancing in what was known as Operation Charnwood. British and Canadian troops reached their objectives on the north bank of the River Orne but much of the city had been destroyed.

Two piers are all that remain from a bridge on the Loire destroyed by Allied aircraft to prevent the movement of German reinforcements.

A canal bridge destroyed in a raid by RAF bombers to prevent German forces retreating across the canal from Caen to Vaucelles.

A site in the Pas de Calais region thought to be connected with the German rocket programme, which was attacked by Bomber Command on 17 July, and again on 20 July.

A V-1 Flying Bomb is wheeled tail-first out of the concrete building where it has been stored, the camouflage nets covering the entrance drawn aside like curtains to allow it to pass.

Anti-aircraft gunners race to man their positions in a battery of Bofors guns on the South Coast of England as the alert sounds to indicate incoming Flying Bombs.

On 16 July, a P-61 Black Widow night fighter of the 422nd Night Fighter Squadron intercepted and destroyed a V-1, the type's first kill in the European theatre. Armed with four 20-mm cannon and four .50 calibre machine guns and carrying a crew of three, and two Pratt & Whitney Twin Wasp engines, the Black Widow was a radar-equipped night fighter that served widely with the US forces from 1944.

Barrage balloons were the last line of defence against the V-1 Flying Bombs. At one point, almost 2,000 balloons were positioned to the south-east of London to counter low-flying V-1s. This photograph shows part of the barrage.

The site of a barrage balloon credited with being the first to bring down a Flying Bomb. The wreckage in the foreground shows where the V-1 landed on what had previously been a barn.

On 26 July, an RAF Mosquito reconnaissance aircraft was attacked and damaged by a Luftwaffe Me 262 in what was the first aerial victory for a jet. This photograph shows one of the early Me 262 test beds; the Me 262 had had a long gestation period. (John Christopher Collection)

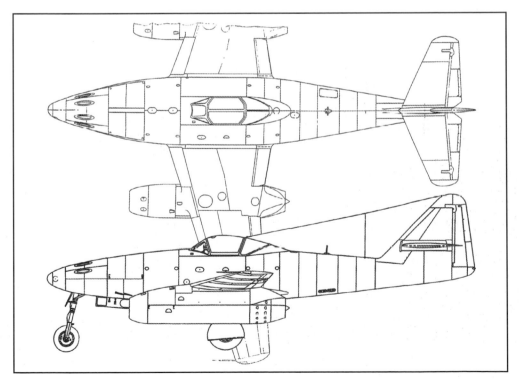

The Me 262 had been under development since mid-1939 but only came into service when a special unit was formed to fly it in April. A swept-wing aircraft powered by two Junkers Jumo 004 turbojets, the Me 262 was faster than any Allied fighter and heavily armed with four 30-mm cannon. (John Christopher Collection)

On 17 July, it was reported that a force of eight Soviet Yakovlev Yak-3 fighters attacked sixty Luftwaffe aircraft, shooting down three Junkers Ju 87 Stuka dive bombers and four Messerschmitt Bf 109 G escort fighters for no losses of their own.

RAF Bristol Beaufighters mount a low-level attack on a German supply convoy off the coast of Norway. Two of the Beaufighters can be seen in the middle of the photograph, flying not much higher than the masts of the ship they are attacking.

August

On 5 August, a force of RAF Lancasters modified to carry the 12,000-lb Tallboy earthquake bombs attacked the reinforced concrete U-boat pens at Brest in the far west of France.

A photograph taken from inside one of the U-boat pens following the capture of Brest in September 1944. This hole gives an idea of the strength of the construction of the U-boat pens.

On 12 August, production of the Hawker Hurricane, one of the most famous British aircraft of the Second World War, was ended. This photograph shows the last aircraft to leave the factory. The banner records some of the battles and theatres of the war where Hurricanes had served.

Waco gliders carrying American airborne troops litter these fields in southern France on the morning of 12 August. The airborne troops landed in support of an invasion force attacking the coast between Nice and Marseilles.

Hundreds of paratroopers descend over Provence as part of the invasion of the south of France.

American paratroopers in a C-47 transport on their way to the South of France.

Allied armour moves along the country roads of Normandy towards the front line near Falaise while an RAF Mustang patrols overhead.

German troops and vehicles trying to escape towards the Seine and out of the Falaise pocket, in which elements of the German Seventh Army and Fifth Panzer Armies were encircled. To the bottom left of the photograph, vehicles can be seen trying to pass around a large bomb crater in the road.

A rocket fired from a Typhoon fighter bomber speeds towards a vehicle on the road near Falaise. After Falaise, the 17th SS Panzer Division had lost 94 per cent of its armour and 70 per cent of its vehicles.

Two American soldiers are seen beside a railway locomotive, the boiler of which has exploded spectacularly after having been hit in an air attack.

A German barracks outside the town of Egletons, south-east of Limoges, gives off a cloud of smoke after being bombed by RAF Mosquitoes.

Rockets fired by RAF Bristol Beaufighters flying from Italy explode on a building in Dubrovnik, on the coast of what is now Croatia, which was thought to be a headquarters for the German forces fighting Tito's partisans.

Two spotters on a London roof top watch the flight of a V-1 Flying Bomb as it approaches the capital, ready to give the alarm and warn people to take cover.

A spectacular photograph showing a night-time barrage of anti-aircraft fire as V-1s are detected inbound over southern England.

Opposite: A V-1 launch site at Fontaine-sous-Préaux, outside Rouen, which had been hit by a bomb just as a Flying Bomb had been about to be launched, is examined by a soldier.

Two close-up views showing an RAF incendiary bomb and its effects. The bomb itself weighed 30 lb and, as can be seen in the other photograph, shoots out a 15-foot jet of flame for two minutes.

A photograph taken during an attack on a U-boat which earned the pilot of the attacking aircraft, a Consolidated Catalina flying boat, the VC for continuing the attack despite having been wounded seventy-two times.

September

An air raid by US Marauders and Havocs on the port of Brest on 3 September. Brest was garrisoned by German Fallschirmjäger and the bombing and artillery barrages required to destroy their fortifications meant that the old city of Brest was almost entirely destroyed by the time the Germans surrendered on 19 September.

Like Brest, Le Havre, home of a German naval base, was bombed very heavily prior to its liberation, as this photograph showed. The French Atlantic and Channel ports were vital objectives for the Allies to keep up the flow of supplies to the armies in the field.

A 150-mm gun mounted on a railway carriage bed that had been attacked and destroyed in Montreuil in the Pas de Calais region of northern France by RAF aircraft.

A V-1 Flying Bomb which
had crashed in a field not
long after being launched
is examined by a Canadian
sergeant and a member of
the Resistance.

The Spitfire Mk XIV, which
was powered by a 2,000 hp
Rolls-Royce Griffon engine,
was first flown in October
1943 and was the Spitfire
variant that was most
successfully used to intercept
V-1 Flying Bombs.

A V-1 launch site at Belloy-sur-Somme, northern France, put out of action by the Germans as Allied forces advanced.

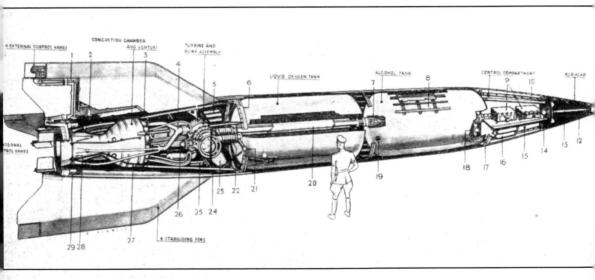

The V-2 rocket first saw action on 8 September, when a single rocket hit Paris. Later that same day, another rocket landed in Chiswick, west London, killing three people. This cutaway diagram shows the scale and some of the key parts of the V-2.

Above: Photographs showing parts from a wrecked V-2 rocket found in Belgium. These two photographs show the rocket's jet engine and the tank for the hydrogen peroxide used to provide the steam that drove the turbine powering the fuel and oxidiser pumps.

Right: Handley Page Halifaxes towing Horsa gliders full of airborne troops towards the Rhine on 17 September, the first day of the ill-fated Operation Market Garden.

Above: This photograph shows
something of the scale of the airborne
assault launched in Operation Market
Garden: clouds of paratroopers are
seen descending onto a drop zone in the
Netherlands.

Left: Heavily laden American
paratroopers pose on the steps of their
transport plane prior to setting off on
Operation Market Garden.

This map of Germany and the Low Countries shows the drive mounted by XXX Corps towards the British paratroopers on the Rhine at Arnhem.

On 20 September, Lancaster and Halifax bombers of the RAF launched a heavy attack against Calais, flying at altitudes as low as 2,000 or 1,500 feet. Calais, the heavily fortified German headquarters for the Pas de Calais region, the area immediately opposite Dover where the Germans thought the Allied invasion most likely, was another of the Channel ports needed by the Allies to maintain their supply lines and was liberated over a period of about a week from 25 September.

A B-17 of the US Eighth Air Force is seen above Ludwigshafen during one of the many attacks on the city's chemical industry that were intended to stop the production of German synthetic oil.

Opposite: On the night of 23/24 September, 617 Squadron attacked the Dortmund–Ems Canal with 12,000-lb Tallboy earthquake bombs designed by Barnes Wallis. In this photograph, the two points marked 'A' are direct hits from the Tallboys while 'B' marks where the water drained out of the canal after the banks were broken. 'C' shows the River Slane, which has been camouflaged.

Paratroopers from the British 1st Airborne Division, evacuated over the Rhine after the end of Operation Market Garden, pose for a photograph.

Smoke pouring from a Japanese oil facility at Boela on the island of Ceram, in what is now Indonesia, after an attack by USAAF bombers flying from bases in northern Australia.

October

On 3 October, RAF Lancasters bombed a dyke on the Dutch island of Walcheren, allowing the sea to flood a large part of the island. Walcheren, at the mouth of the River Scheldt, controlled access to the Port of Antwerp. The flooding forced the German defenders to evacuate the central part of the island.

On 5 October, the Ruhr town of Saarbrücken was bombed heavily by the RAF at the request of the US Army, to disrupt German supply lines. The River Saar can be seen at the top of the photograph, and the devastated railway station in the lower half of the image.

An RAF officer examines pieces of the first German jet fighter to be brought down, a Me 262 shot down by six Spitfires over the Dutch city of Nijmegen on 5 October.

Two images of the Hawker Tempest. The Tempest, armed with four 20-mm cannon, was fast and manoeuvrable and used both for ground attack (carrying bombs and rockets like its close cousin the Hawker Typhoon) and to intercept V-1 Flying Bombs and Me 262 jet fighters, attacking the latter at low level as they came into land.

On 7 October, Lancasters of 617 Squadron led by the squadron's commander, James Tait, attacked the Kembs dam on the Rhine north of Basel at low level using 12,000-lb Tallboy earthquake bombs and made a breach in the dam. There had been concerns that the water could have been released to obstruct advancing American troops.

A meeting between General Joseph Stillwell (left), the American commander of the Chinese forces, and Curtis LeMay (right), commander of XX Bomber Command, which included the B-29s flying from China. They are seen on one of the B-29 bases 'somewhere in China'. (LoC)

On 14 October, there were air raids on the heavily-bombed city of Cologne by both RAF Mosquitoes and aircraft of the US Eighth Air Force. Bombs dropped by the American force are thought to have destroyed the Mulheim suspension bridge across the Rhine.

On 14 October, British paratroopers landed at Megara airfield west of Athens. The lefthand image shows the paratroopers descending and the upper image shows the paratroopers fanning out through the olive trees outside the airfield.

US and British carrier aircraft form up at daybreak for a raid to attack Japanese shipping and naval and air bases in the Dutch East Indies, now Indonesia.

A Corsair fighter damaged during a raid on a Japanese base at Sigli, on the island of Sumatra, lands back on its aircraft carrier on 18 September.

Black smoke rises from the sea, showing where a Japanese bomber has been shot down while attacking the aircraft carrier USS *Princeton* off the Philippines on 24 October. Another US aircraft carrier is seen to the right, manoeuvring to avoid more aircraft.

Spray from an exploding bomb can be seen covering part of the US aircraft carrier in the background of this photograph, while in the foreground the guns of the aircraft carrier on which the photographer is standing are opening fire on the bombers.

An artist's impression of an attack mounted by Lancasters of 617 Squadron and 9 Squadron against the German battleship *Tirpitz*. Cloud cover obscured the battleship although one of the 12,000-lb Tallboy bombs dropped by the Lancasters was a near miss.

A map of Saarbrücken, in the west of Germany, marking areas of visible damage in black following a raid by RAF Bomber Command on 29 October.

On 31 October, a force of twenty-four Mosquitoes again carried out a low-level precision bombing raid, this time attacking a Gestapo headquarters in Denmark housed in part of the University of Aarhus in the north of Jutland. This photograph was taken from one of the Mosquitoes as the raid was carried out.

November

Armourers loading a de Havilland Mosquito with cannon shells. Mosquito night fighters like this were used as escorts for bombing raids over Germany. Those flown by the RAF's 100 Group were fitted with devices to track the German IFF (Identification Friend or Foe) systems and their Lichtenstein radars.

Two photographs showing the wreckage of houses hit by German V-2 rockets.

The crater caused by the explosion of a V-2 rocket.

Left: The rocket trail from a V-2, photographed by a very surprised USAAF pilot whose aircraft it flashed past. Another American aircraft, which had been flying in formation with the photographer's aircraft, is seen ringed to the bottom right of the photograph.

Top: Another of the variants of the almost endlessly flexible Mosquito. This model, the Mk XVIII, carried four machine guns and a 6-lb gun and was used by the RAF's Coastal Command in attacks on enemy shipping.

Above: An RAF Halifax drops supplies for Marshal Tito's partisans in Yugoslavia, the drop zone marked by smoke.

Although many joined the RAF thinking that it would be a better option than the Army, it could still be very hard work as this photograph of ground crew pushing a trailer of bombs across a heavily waterlogged airfield in the Netherlands shows.

The solution to another problem found on airfields in liberated Europe. This photograph shows a magnetic device known as the Snifter that was used to pick up pieces of metal such as bomb fragments that had been damaging aircraft tyres.

A sergeant of the USAAF packing a parachute at a US bomber base in the UK. 'If it doesn't work, bring it back and we'll give you another one,' was the old joke between the parachute packers and the air crew.

Another vital piece of kit for many bomber crews, both RAF and USAAF, was the inflatable dinghy, into which the crew could escape if a damaged aircraft came down in the North Sea or the English Channel. This photograph shows a British model of a dinghy carried by US aircraft being inspected by an American lieutenant and corporal.

On 12 November, Lancaster bombers of 617 Squadron and 9 Squadron finally succeeded in sinking the German battleship *Tirpitz*. Flying from bases in the northern Soviet Union, the pilots used 12,000-lb Tallboy earthquake bombs designed by Barnes Wallis to capsize *Tirpitz*. These two photographs show the raid underway, with smoke pouring from the battleship.

Above: In this photograph of the different bombs used by RAF Bomber Command, the 12,000-lb Tallboy can be seen at the back. The two airmen standing behind it give a sense of the size of the bomb.

Opposite top: Wing-Commander James Tait, the commander of 617 Squadron, who led the attack against the *Tirpitz*.

Opposite middle and bottom: RAF Coastal Command aircraft used powerful flares to illuminate targets when attacking at night, particularly in the winter months. These two photographs show ground crew loading flares into a rack ready to be placed into the bomb bay of a Vickers Wellington of what was known as the Shipfinder Force, while the upper photograph shows a Bristol Beaufighter of Coastal Command on a coastal airfield silhouetted by flares dropped at sea.

An RAF Liberator bomber with a load of bombs stretching out in front of it on an airfield in India. This aircraft would take part, later in the day, in a daylight bombing raid on the railways and docks of Rangoon, in Japanese-occupied Burma.

December

British paratroopers hurry across an Athens street as they attempt to quell disturbances in the Greek capital in early December.

A spectacular photograph taken at night at the base of an RAF Mosquito squadron. The de Havilland Mosquito FB Mk VI, pictured here, could carry four 500-lb bombs and, as seen here, was armed with four 20-mm cannon and four machine guns, which is seen testing.

Waiting to give the Mosquito pilots their take-off signal, this sergeant holds up an Aldis signal lamp.

Two vivid photographs taken from an attack made by Bristol Beaufighters of the RAF and SAAF flying from Italy against barracks and houses occupied by German troops in a village in Yugoslavia. In the top photograph, rockets are seen flying towards the target, and in the bottom smoke is rising from the village.

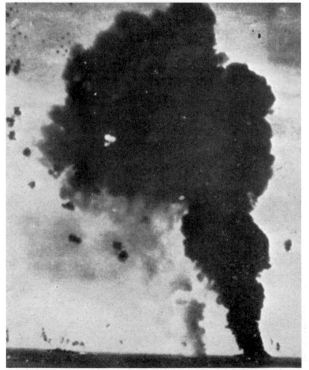

Deck crew on board a Royal Navy aircraft carrier move a Fairey Barracuda torpedo bomber that has just returned from an air raid on the Indonesian island of Padang just off Sumatra.

A vast column of black smoke rises from a US Navy destroyer hit by a bomb in the Leyte Gulf in the Philippines. The white smoke beside it comes from a destroyed aircraft.

Manila harbour, obscured by smoke
from ships hit during an air raid by
American carrier-borne aircraft.

A B-29 Supertortress takes off from a
base on the island of Saipan for a raid.

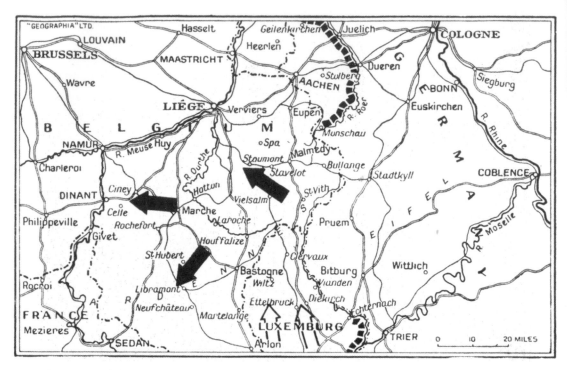

The Battle of the Bulge. This map shows the initial German advance through the Ardennes towards the River Meuse.

Bad weather along the Western Front gave the advancing Germans the advantage and prevented the Allied air forces from intervening during the first part of the Battle of the Bulge. This photograph shows RAF ground crew struggling to move a 1,000-lb bomb through thick mud.

The Luftwaffe put up a strong effort to support the Battle of the Bulge but suffered losses that it could very ill afford. Here, American troops examine the wreckage of a Fw 190 brought down close to the German border.

Troops of the US 101st Airborne Division man an anti-aircraft gun in the snow outside Bastogne, watching the sky for signs of German aircraft.

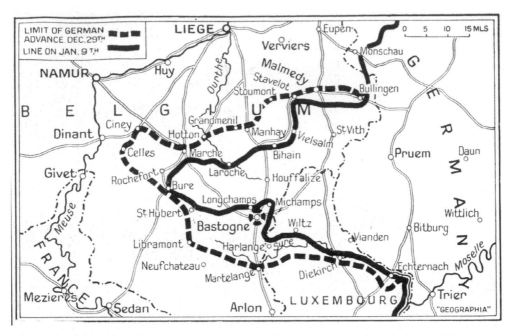

The Battle of the Bulge, showing the German front lines on 29 December, the limit of the German advance, and on 9 January 1945 after the Allies had counter-attacked.

C-47 transport aircraft circle over a drop zone at Bastogne as supplies are dropped to the besieged American troops holding the town.

American troops besieged in Bastogne examine boxes of ammunition and other supplies dropped to them by parachute.

RAF Lancaster and Halifax bombers attack St Vith, an important supply base for the German forces advancing through the Ardennes, on 26 December.

Ground crew in a squadron of the Second Tactical Air Force at a Typhoon squadron on an airbase in the Netherlands rolling a 1,000-lb bomb while more ground crew are servicing one of the aircraft in the background.